Rosalind
FRANKLIN

Cath Senker

an imprint of Hodder Children's Books

© 2002 White-Thomson Publishing Ltd

Produced for Hodder Wayland by
White-Thomson Publishing Ltd
2/3 St Andrew's Place
Lewes
BN7 1UP

Editor: Anna Lee
Designer: Malcolm Walker
Picture Researcher: Shelley Noronha, Glass Onion Pictures
Science Panel Illustrator: Nick Hawken
Map Illustrator: Tim Mayer
Consultant: Dr Brian Bowers, Senior Research Fellow
at the Science Museum, London
Proofreader: Philippa Smith

Cover and title page: a portrait of Rosalind Franklin.

Published in Great Britain in 2002 by Hodder Wayland,
an imprint of Hodder Children's Books.

British Library Cataloguing in Publication Data
Senker, Cath
Rosalind Franklin. – (Scientists who made history)
1. Franklin, Rosalind 2. Women molecular biologists –
Biography – Juvenile literature 3. Molecular biologists –
Biography – Juvenile literature 4. DNA – History –
Juvenile literature
I. Title II. Lee, Anna
572.8'6'092

ISBN 0 7502 4005 9

Printed and bound in Italy by G. Canale & C.S.p.A., Turin

Hodder Children's Books
A division of Hodder Headline Limited
338 Euston Road, London, NW1 3BH

Picture Acknowledgements: Camera Press 11, 13, 23; Hulton Archive 6;
Jenifer Glynn 9, 18, 19, 29, 34, 36b, 37; Mary Evans Picture Library
21t, 22, 30; Newnham College, Cambridge *cover, title page*, 4;
Popperfoto 8, 10, 12, 20, 26, 35, 38, 39, 41, 42; Science and Society
Picture Library 14, 15, 17, 31; Science Photo Library 5, 21b, 25, 26,
27, 28, 32, 33, 36t, 43; Topham Picturepoint 7, 40.

Acknowledgements: The author would like to thank the following
for their help in writing this book: Michael Cardona, Nicola
Hardwick and Dr Jacky Senker. I am especially grateful to Jenifer
Glynn, Rosalind Franklin's sister, and her husband Professor Ian
Glynn for helping to answer queries and providing photographs.
The panel on page 17 is adapted from *The Extraordinary Chemistry
of Ordinary Things*, 3rd edition, by Carl H. Snyder. A main source
for this book was *Rosalind Franklin and DNA* by Anne Sayre
(Norton, 2000).

Contents

The Secret of Life

The moment of triumph

IT IS FEBRUARY 1953. Brilliant young scientist Rosalind Franklin is working hard in her laboratory at King's College, London. She's excited. After two years of difficult, close-up work on tiny pieces of deoxyribonucleic acid – DNA – she realizes she is finally close to finding out what it looks like and how it is constructed. This will be a fantastic discovery. DNA is at the root of all human beings. It contains genes, which are passed on from our parents and help to make us the people we are.

LEFT: *A portrait of Rosalind Franklin. Many people today think only of Crick and Watson as the scientists who worked out the structure of DNA, but Franklin played a vital role.*

LEFT: *James Watson (left) and Francis Crick (right), with their model of part of a DNA molecule in 1953. They had tried to put the model together in many different ways before they came up with the correct solution.*

At Cambridge University a bright pair of scientists, Francis Crick and James Watson, are attempting to crack the same problem. They have spent months trying to come up with a correct model for the structure (the size and shape) of DNA. Yet they haven't done any experiments to give evidence for their models. Without evidence, they cannot prove anything.

Help is at hand for the pair. They manage to obtain Rosalind Franklin's data, without her knowing. They joyfully discover it gives them most of the evidence they need. Soon, the solution to the final piece of the puzzle comes to Watson and he dashes to the laboratory to tell Crick. A couple of days later, on 28 February, they come up with a model that looks perfect.

On 17 March Franklin finishes a scientific paper with her DNA results so far. The following day, Crick and Watson's triumphant paper arrives at King's College from Cambridge. The mystery of DNA is solved, and the glory will go to the two men. Franklin will never know just how much of her own work has gone into this amazing achievement.

IN THEIR OWN WORDS

'At lunch Francis winged in to the Eagle [a pub in Cambridge] to tell everyone within hearing distance that we had found the secret of life.'

JAMES WATSON, *THE DOUBLE HELIX*, 1968.

WOMEN IN BRITAIN IN THE 1920S

Franklin was born in 1920, during a period of great change for women in Britain. Many had taken on important work during the First World War (1914–1918). Some were nurses at the battlefront. Many replaced men who had joined the armed forces, working in weapons factories, offices or in other jobs previously done by men. After the war, many wanted to keep their new independence. They wanted more rights.

In 1918, after a big campaign, the British government finally gave women householders aged over 30 the right to vote. Ten years later all women over 21 were given this right.

IN THEIR OWN WORDS

'Time was when I thought men alone maintained the State. Now I know that the modern State must be dependent on women and men alike.'

WELL-KNOWN BRITISH JOURNALIST,
J. L. GARVIN, 1917.

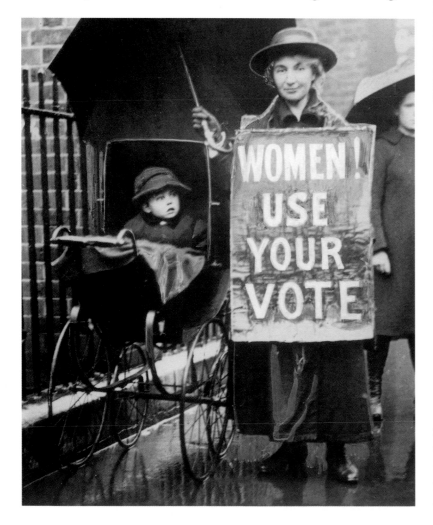

LEFT: *A mother urging other women to use their voting rights in 1925. The position of women in Britain changed dramatically after the First World War.*

Economic changes brought new opportunities for women. New factories were being built to make electrical goods, for example. Young unmarried women went out to work to earn their own money, so they did not have to depend on their families for everything. In 1931, one third of women were employed outside the home. They enjoyed their new freedom, dressing comfortably in shorter skirts, and going out with their friends after work.

For working-class women, a job made a big difference to the family's income. Yet women from well-off families were not expected to work for a living. They didn't need to – although they might do charity work in their spare time. A good education was important so that they could bring up their children well. But their main job was still to look after the family and home. Franklin was to have a very different sort of life from most women of her generation.

ABOVE: *Factory workers making electrical goods in 1938-9. Women worked for money, which in turn gave them greater independence. Yet they did not receive equal pay and were not treated equally to men. In some jobs, such as in teaching and the Civil Service, they had to leave if they married.*

A Clever Young Woman

ROSALIND FRANKLIN WAS born in London on
25 July 1920, the second child in a happy family. Her
parents, Muriel and Ellis, came from a wealthy Jewish
background. Both their families were heavily involved in
social work, helping the Jewish community and poor people.
The women of the family took part, too. Rosalind's father
had wanted to study science, but fighting in the war and his
early marriage made this impossible. Instead, he became a
successful banker.

Muriel and Ellis went on to have three more children.
There were two girls and three boys. Rosalind's parents
treated their sons and daughters equally, which was unusual
in the 1920s. They were all given a good education and
brought up to think for themselves.

BELOW: *London Bridge,
London, looking across to
Adelaide House, in the 1920s.
Rosalind was born in London
and spent most of her life there.*

ABOVE: *Franklin (second from right) with (from left) her brothers Colin and David, her sister Jenifer and her youngest brother, Roland.*

Rosalind was an intelligent and logical little girl, who was always asking questions. She loved drawing and making things and wasn't interested in dolls. Construction toys were her favourite. When Muriel and Ellis set up a carpenter's workbench for the children to use, it was Rosalind who spent the most time there.

When she was nine, Rosalind became ill. She was sent away to a boarding school by the sea for a year or so. She hated it there and grew determined never to give in to illness again. Her secondary school was St Paul's Girls' School, where the physics and chemistry courses were just as good as those in boys' schools. Many students went on to good careers, and Rosalind hoped to follow in their footsteps.

IN THEIR OWN WORDS

'We spent the whole arithmetic lesson today with a lovely discussion about gravity and all that sort of stuff.'

ROSALIND FRANKLIN, AGED THIRTEEN.

'I Want to be a Scientist'

By the age of fifteen Rosalind Franklin knew she wanted to be a scientist. Three years later, in 1938, she started at Newnham College for women, at Cambridge University. In those days, men and women could not go to the same college. The rules at Cambridge were unfair. No more than 500 women were allowed to attend the university at one time. Yet in October 1935, for example, there were 5,328 male students. Furthermore, women were not awarded proper degrees, equal to men's, until 1948.

However, Franklin met some wonderful role models at Newnham. She was taught physics and chemistry by women teachers with successful careers. Some of these professional women were even married with children. This was rare in those days.

BELOW: *Sidgwick Hall, part of Newnham College, Cambridge, pictured after the Second World War. There were two colleges for women at Cambridge at this time. Only girls from wealthy families were able to go to good schools and continue their studies at university.*

'Practically the whole of the Cavendish [Cambridge science laboratory scientists] have [sic] disappeared [into war research]... [Before the war] biochemistry was almost entirely run by Germans and may not survive.'

LETTER FROM ROSALIND FRANKLIN TO HER PARENTS ABOUT HER UNIVERSITY STUDIES, 12 OCTOBER 1940. [GERMANS WHO REMAINED IN BRITAIN DURING THE WAR WERE PUT IN PRISON FOR POLITICAL REASONS.]

ABOVE: *Scientists signing up for the Second World War in 1940. Many universities had to make do with fewer teachers during the war years.*

The Second World War

In 1939, during Franklin's second year at Cambridge, the Second World War broke out. Many good scientists left to do research to help the war effort, leaving few teachers. This meant students had to be more independent, which suited Franklin well.

However, the dangers of war were close, since it was possible that Cambridge would be bombed. Each time there was an air-raid warning, everyone had to go into bomb shelters. Parties, dances and picnics on the river were few and far between in the war years, and student life was rather dull. In the holidays, Franklin worked to help Jewish refugees from Europe who had escaped the war.

SCHOLARSHIP STUDENT

Franklin studied so hard for her final exams at Cambridge that she wore herself out. Exhausted and nervous, she didn't perform as well as she'd hoped. She received a high second – the second highest grade possible – but not the first she had hoped for. She learnt a valuable lesson for life – never wear yourself out completely.

Despite her grade, Newnham College recognized Franklin's talents and offered her a research scholarship so she could do a second degree. Her supervisor was Ronald Norrish, and the two did not get on well. Norrish was known to be a difficult man; the writers of his biography later described him as an obstinate person who did not like to be criticized. Norrish saw his student as highly intelligent, but thought she was 'stubborn and difficult to supervise'.

RIGHT: *The library of Newnham College, where Franklin spent many hours studying.*

Making friends

Although work had its problems, Franklin had a great social life. She made friends with scientist Adrienne Weill, a French refugee who was working at Newnham during the war. Weill rented a house in Cambridge so she could have student lodgers. Franklin helped to prepare it, and in 1941 left her college room and moved in herself. She loved her new independence. Weill's house was always full of interesting people having lively discussions in a mixture of French and English.

Franklin often talked to Weill about what it meant to be a woman scientist. Franklin wasn't an active feminist, fighting for women's rights. She simply wanted people to take her seriously and treat her equally as a scientist.

In 1942 she decided to leave her research post because her experiments were not going well and she could not persuade Norrish to change his approach. Also, she wanted to do something useful in the war. This turned out to be a smart move.

BELOW: *Roland Norrish, Franklin's supervisor at Newnham. Their difficult relationship was part of the reason she decided to leave Cambridge.*

IN THEIR OWN WORDS

'As long as one stays in a university... it is science for knowledge. I'm so afraid that in industry I should find only science for money.'

ROSALIND FRANKLIN IN A LETTER TO HER PARENTS, 1941 OR 1942.

The Holes in Coal

In 1942, just one month after her twenty-second birthday, Franklin was given the job of assistant research officer at the British Coal Utilization Research Association (known as CURA) in London. CURA was an industrial organization that researched the use of coal. As fuel was so important during the war, Franklin knew she would be helping the war effort by working there. She also worked as an air-raid warden in Putney, London.

CURA had been founded in 1938. It grew rapidly during the early years of the Second World War and there were many bright young people like Franklin working there. CURA's buildings were bombed early in the war, so the staff had to move to various workplaces around London.

BELOW: *This street in Islington, North London, has been damaged in a German air raid, 8 September 1944. Luckily, the street shelters (centre) stayed standing. Franklin did voluntary work during the war as an air-raid warden, helping people to find the shelters during an air raid.*

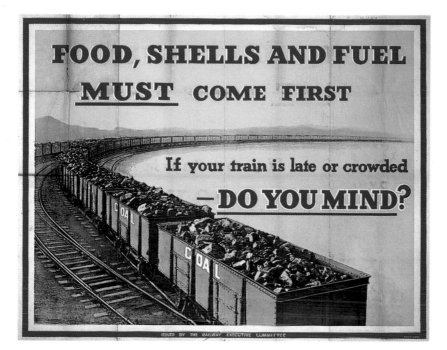

FOOD, SHELLS AND FUEL
MUST COME FIRST

If your train is late or crowded

— DO YOU MIND?

ISSUED BY THE RAILWAY EXECUTIVE COMMITTEE

ABOVE: *A wartime poster showing a goods train loaded with coal, a vital source of fuel. The people at CURA worked to find out how to make the best use of precious coal.*

As the CURA buildings were spread across London, and full of young people, it was a relaxed place to work. Franklin was able to do independent research. Her job was to find out how the structure of coal changes when it is heated.

Franklin worked incredibly hard. Between 1942 and 1946 she had her name on five scientific papers, and had written three of these alone. She also finished her PhD, based on her CURA work, in 1945. At CURA her personality developed and her confidence grew. She sewed bright patch pockets on her lab coat because it looked so dull. More importantly, when CURA put up signs saying that only machine-shop workers could make equipment in the machine shop, Franklin cheerfully turned the sign around and continued to work there.

By 1946 the war was over and at last it was possible to travel again. Franklin felt it was time for a change.

A Scientist in France

ADRIENNE WEILL HAD a useful contact for Franklin. Weill's friend Marcel Mathieu found her a job with the Central State Chemistry Laboratories in Paris. Franklin moved there in February 1947. After the war, France was suffering from food shortages and electricity cuts, and Franklin's salary was small. But she didn't mind not having much money. She was happy with simple food and third-class train travel.

X-ray crystallography

Franklin's job in Paris involved learning X-ray crystallography from Jacques Méring. She had to learn to experiment on tiny materials that were extremely difficult to work with. X-ray crystallography was a relatively new science.

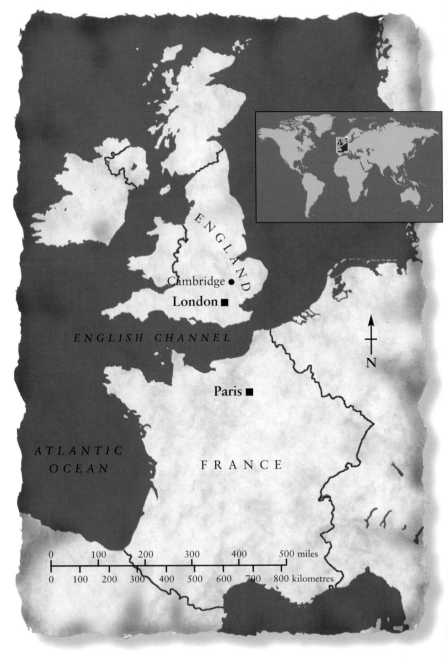

RIGHT: *This map shows the places in which Franklin lived and worked.*

It was first used by a German scientist, Friedrich Knipping, in 1912. X-rays can pass through substances that aren't transparent. This allows you to see inside them. Knipping found that when he passed a beam of X-rays through a crystal (a small piece of a substance with many even sides), the beam formed a pattern on a photographic plate. From the pattern he could work out how the atoms were arranged in the crystal. This helped scientists to find out about the structure of substances that were incredibly minute, far too small to see with a microscope.

BELOW: *A photograph of Professor Dorothy Hodgkin (1910–1994) in the 1940s. An extremely successful X-ray crystallographer, Hodgkin used X-ray photographs to work out the atomic structure of penicillin, vitamin B^{12} and insulin. In 1964, she was awarded the Nobel Prize for chemistry. Hodgkin was the third woman to receive that prize.*

MOLECULES AND ATOMS

All things around us are made up of molecules. This experiment will help you to understand what they are.

Take a pile of paper clips, all the same size and colour. Divide the pile into two equal piles. Keep dividing the piles until you have many single paper clips. One paper clip still does the job of a paper clip – holding loose papers together. Now, imagine that you could cut that one paper clip in half. Could it still do the job of a paper clip? The single paper clip is like a molecule – the smallest part of something, which can't be divided any more without changing what it does.

A molecule is made up of two or more even tinier things called atoms. For example, a molecule of water is made from two atoms of hydrogen and one atom of oxygen (see below). If you break down a water molecule into hydrogen and oxygen, it won't be water any more.

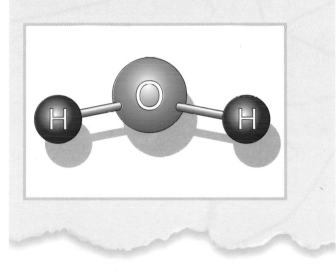

A BLOOMING PERSONALITY

In Paris, Franklin worked in a large, airy laboratory with people from different countries. They all argued loudly about work, politics and everything else under the sun. In their free time they went out for dinner and picnics, and took camping trips together.

Franklin's French practice with Weill and her friends during her years at Cambridge came in useful, and she soon spoke French fluently. She felt at ease in Paris. It was a good atmosphere for intellectuals – people who love learning. In France, intellectuals were not cut off from the rest of society as they seemed to be in England. Instead, they were deeply involved in it.

BELOW: *Rosalind Franklin giving a lecture in Paris, in about 1947. Franklin loved living and working in Paris.*

ABOVE: *Franklin on holiday in Europe, about 1950. An energetic walker and climber, she loved hiking in France and Italy. She would happily do a 16-hour trek, and was quite content to stay in youth hostels.*

Life was easier for an educated woman in France, too. Franklin felt positively welcomed and was treated as an equal. She made good friends with the people she worked with, especially with Vittorio Luzzati and his wife Denise. Her strong personality blossomed – Franklin was no shy little English mouse. She joined in the gossip and discussions around her. She blew up in anger from time to time, like everyone else. In Paris, Franklin was seen as a real character.

These years, from early 1947 until the end of 1950, were perhaps the happiest times of Franklin's life. Yet although she loved life in Paris, she decided to go back to London. In the late 1940s, the improvements in X-ray crystallography made it possible to try it out on molecules from living things. This was a fascinating new area of scientific research, and it was happening in London. Franklin was keen to take up the challenge.

IN THEIR OWN WORDS

'From the evidence of her letters, the reasons were personal, a feeling that after four years it was time to decide whether her future lay permanently in France. It was not easy, and she was full of last-minute doubts.'

FRANKLIN'S SISTER, JENIFER GLYNN (1996), ABOUT FRANKLIN'S DECISION TO LEAVE FRANCE IN 1950.

The DNA Problem

An exciting opportunity

PROFESSOR JOHN RANDALL of King's College, London, had specially invited Franklin to come and work for him. She started her new job at King's at the beginning of 1951.

Randall wanted Franklin to build an X-ray crystallography unit within his laboratory. He hoped that crystallography would help scientists to find out about genes.

It is genes that make all living things what they are. For example, all humans share many features. We have blood, lungs, a large brain, and we walk on two legs. However, there are certain things about people that they share with their family in particular. For example, you may look like your mum, or be left-handed like your dad. This is because many features are passed on to you from your parents through the genes.

LEFT: *Henrik (right) and Daniel (left) Sedin play ice hockey for the Vancouver Canucks. They are identical twins, which means they share exactly the same genes. They look similar and may behave in a similar way, but there can be differences too. Other influences, such as a person's surroundings and way of life, affect them as well as their genes.*

LEFT: *US scientist Alfred Day Hershey. In 1952, he and fellow scientist Martha Chase carried out experiments that proved that the genes are found in DNA.*

In 1950, people didn't know exactly how this happened. Between the mid-1920s and mid-1940s, scientists had done many experiments. They had discovered that genes are in DNA, which is found in the cells of plants and animals.

In order to discover how the genes worked, scientists had to do more research on DNA. They needed to know its structure and how the atoms joined up to form the DNA. It was Franklin's job to find out.

CELLS AND DNA

Your body is made up of a 100 million million cells. That's 100,000,000,000,000! The largest cells are about as wide as a human hair, but most are smaller. Your little toe might have two or three thousand million cells, depending on how big it is.

The genes are in the DNA, which is coiled up in the cells of living things. DNA can be several millimetres long, but is only 0.000002 mm wide! So now you can imagine just how tricky it was for Franklin to work on DNA.

ABOVE: *This photograph shows a cross-section (slice through the middle) of a hair follicle, the place where a hair is joined to the head. It is shown 100 times its real size so you can see the tiny cells clearly.*

A WOMAN AT KING'S COLLEGE

When Franklin arrived at King's College, Maurice Wilkins, a scientist from New Zealand, was already trying to discover the structure of DNA. Professor Randall did not make it clear to him that Franklin was also going to be taking on DNA research. A meeting was held to discuss Franklin's role in the DNA project, but Wilkins was away. He returned to find that Franklin had taken over part of his job. This created an awkward situation.

Wilkins and Franklin did not get on well from the first moment they met. They had different styles of working. Franklin loved loud, fiery discussions about science, like the ones she'd enjoyed in Paris. Wilkins hated to argue, and if Franklin started a discussion, he just went quiet.

IN THEIR OWN WORDS

'If you believed what you were saying, you had to argue strongly with Rosalind if she thought you were wrong, whereas Maurice would simply shut up.'

RAYMOND GOSLING, IN AN INTERVIEW WITH ROSALIND'S BIOGRAPHER, ANNE SAYRE.

LEFT: *Maurice Wilkins (born in New Zealand, 1916), had been working at King's College for five years when Franklin arrived. Wilkins was just four years older than Franklin and had also been to Cambridge University. They had enough in common to get on well, but unfortunately they disliked each other from the start.*

LEFT: *Professor John Randall, who offered Franklin a fellowship – an award of money to do research – at King's College. There were already several scientists working on the DNA project but they did not have Franklin's skills in X-ray crystallography.*

The atmosphere at King's College was like a men's club. Women were not made welcome, even though several women worked there. (In December 1952, eight out of the thirty-one scientists working for Randall were women.) A comfortable canteen was provided where the men could have lunch; women were not allowed in. The men met up in the pub in the evening to chat about their work and test out their latest ideas. Franklin was left out of these interesting discussions. It was totally different from her experience in Paris.

Franklin found it hard to make friends at King's College and she worked mostly on her own. She did get on very well with Raymond Gosling, her research assistant, but there was no one with her experience to share ideas with or to have the high-level debates that spark off brilliant ideas.

FRANKLIN'S LECTURE AT KING'S

During late 1951 Franklin was cheered by her first big success. She had realized that she could change DNA by wetting it, making a new form called the B form. (The dry form was the A form.) The B form was extremely hard to photograph, though.

Franklin now had important clues about the structure of DNA. She was ready to announce her findings to other people. Researchers like to do this when they are working on new ideas. They want to meet with others to see what they think. Their fellow scientists tell them if their ideas make sense or not.

However, scientists never give away all the details of what they are working on. Quite naturally, they like to publish their new ideas first so that they receive the praise.

THE SHAPE OF DNA

One of the main questions about the DNA molecule was 'What shape is it?' In late 1951, Franklin thought that DNA was in the shape of a helix (near left) but she wasn't sure yet. A helix is a spiral shape. It turned out that DNA was indeed that shape. The DNA molecule has two helices, twisting round each other (far right). This is known as a double helix.

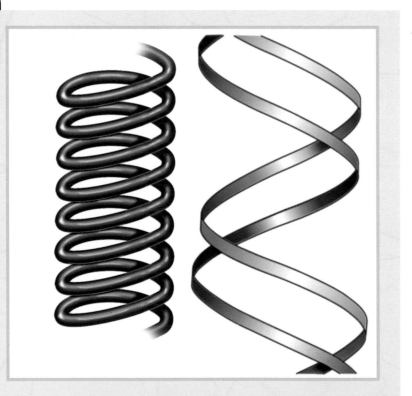

LEFT: *James Watson (born 1928) in Cambridge in 1953. Watson was incredibly bright. He went to the University of Chicago when he was only fifteen and finished his degree at nineteen. By twenty-two he had completed his PhD. In 1951, Watson went to work at the Cavendish Laboratory, Cambridge University.*

In November 1951, Franklin gave a talk to about fifteen people at King's College. One of the things she told them was that she believed the DNA molecule was in the shape of a helix (see panel).

Listening to the lecture was a clever young American scientist called James Watson. He was working at Cambridge University. Watson was excited by the DNA problem. He had gone to the meeting to pick up clues about its structure. Yet it seems that he didn't notice the important ideas in Franklin's talk, for example, that the DNA molecule was a helix.

There was little discussion at the meeting. No one seemed to feel that a big discovery was on the way.

THE RACE THAT NEVER WAS

After hearing Franklin's talk, Watson dashed back to Cambridge. He couldn't wait to tell his friend Francis Crick what he remembered from the talk. Watson and Crick shared a fascination for DNA and were keen to be the first people to discover its structure. British scientist Crick, aged 35, was an outgoing man, bursting with wonderful theories. He was remarkably intelligent. The two made a successful, creative team.

Crick and Watson rushed to make a model of the DNA molecule, hoping that they had solved the puzzle. They invited Franklin and Wilkins to view it. As soon as Franklin saw the model, she pointed out the basic mistakes in it.

ABOVE: *Francis Crick in 1952. He had been unwilling to think about the DNA problem before meeting Watson, because it was Wilkins' and Franklin's job at King's College. But then Watson joined the Cavendish, with his desire to work on DNA. The two began to spend hours each day discussing the question of genes.*

MODEL BUILDING

This is how Crick and Watson worked on the structure of DNA.

1. They used evidence from Rosalind Franklin's photos of DNA, taken using X-ray crystallography, to work out the molecule's shape and size.

2. They used their knowledge of the rules of chemistry. The atoms had to fit together following the rules. For example, there are certain atoms that can go next to each other, and others that can't.

3. They talked to other scientists who knew about DNA, maths and chemistry to get ideas.

4. They made models of the molecule. Crick and Watson used various round shapes for the different kinds of atoms, and pieces of wire to join them together. They put the atoms together in different ways until they found a model that followed all the rules and fitted with all the evidence.

LEFT: *Sir Laurence Bragg (1890–1971), head of the Cavendish Laboratory in the 1950s. He had worked with his father on developing the technique of X-ray crystallography. Bragg shared the 1915 Nobel Prize with his father when he was only 25.*

Laurence Bragg, the head of the Cambridge Laboratory, was furious. Crick and Watson weren't supposed to be working on DNA. There was an agreement with King's College that DNA work would be done there. It was seen as a waste of money for scientists to take on projects that others in their country were already working on. Crick and Watson were breaking the rules, so Bragg banned them from working on DNA.

The pair took no notice. It was quite common for scientists to race against others   often in another country to see who could make a discovery first. They were determined, and wouldn't let the DNA problem rest. For them, the race was on. Franklin, working alone in London, didn't even know there was a race.

The DNA Puzzle Solved

Franklin's progress

AT THE END of 1951 Franklin was feeling depressed and lonely. She was even thinking about giving up the DNA project and leaving King's College. At the start of 1952 she went to talk to scientist John Desmond Bernal at Birkbeck College, London, about a possible job working in his biological group.

Yet her work on DNA was going well. Between January 1951 and June 1952, Franklin was making excellent progress on DNA. In mid-1952, after spending a long time working on the A form of DNA, she realized that she might get some interesting results from the B form. As it turned out, she was right. She managed to take a good photo of the B form of DNA, which clearly showed a helix. This was a great achievement.

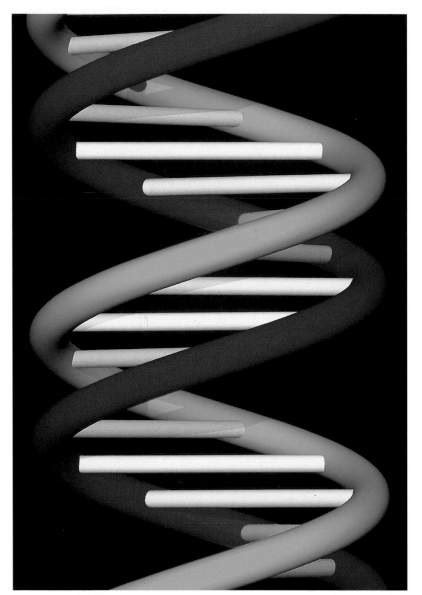

RIGHT: *This modern computer artwork of part of a strand of the B form of DNA shows the two helices spiralling clockwise. Franklin's discovery of the shape of DNA was a big step in DNA research.*

DEFENSE ABSOLUE
de FUMER
DANS LES DORTOIRS

Life in the lab was difficult, though. Franklin's relationship with Maurice Wilkins was worse than ever. The two barely spoke to each other. Although they were both working on DNA at the same time, they didn't discuss their results.

Watson was friendly with Wilkins and used to ask him about Franklin's work. The pair often discussed the DNA question, and Wilkins secretly showed Watson her data. Watson felt sorry for Wilkins. He believed that Franklin was a stubborn woman who should really be working as Wilkins' helper, and not doing her own research.

Despite these problems, Franklin's work continued to progress.

ABOVE: *Franklin in an alpine hut in the early 1950s, during one of her climbing adventures in the Alps. These holidays gave her a break from the problems at work.*

IN THEIR OWN WORDS

'Clearly Rosy had to go or be put in her place.'

JAMES WATSON,
THE DOUBLE HELIX, 1968.

THE BIG RACE

Crick and Watson were not only racing Franklin and Wilkins to solve the DNA question. They were also competing against a great US scientist, Linus Pauling. Like Franklin, Pauling had no idea that he was in a race.

In January 1953, Pauling wrote a paper on the structure of DNA. He sent a copy to his son Peter, who was studying at Cambridge University. Peter Pauling was friendly with Crick and Watson, so he showed it to them straight away.

Crick and Watson quickly read through the paper. They saw immediately that it was totally wrong! Amazed, they realized that if the famous Pauling was on the wrong track, they stood a good chance of beating him to the solution.

A few days later, Watson visited King's College to tell Franklin and Wilkins about Pauling's paper. Without telling Franklin, Wilkins showed Watson her best X-ray photo of the B form of DNA. Watson's jaw dropped as he stared at clear proof that DNA was a helix.

IN THEIR OWN WORDS

'The instant I saw the picture my mouth fell open and my pulse began to race.'

JAMES WATSON ON SEEING FRANKLIN'S PHOTO OF DNA SHOWING A CLEAR HELIX, *THE DOUBLE HELIX*, 1968.

LEFT: *US scientist Linus Pauling (1901–1994). According to his son, Peter Pauling, Linus was interested in DNA but he was not racing against anyone to find out its structure.*

LEFT: *The model showing the structure of DNA that was built by Crick and Watson in 1953. In order to build a model of a molecule, scientists first need to find out a lot of hard facts about the atoms in it.*

Success for Crick and Watson

Back in December 1952, Crick and Watson had obtained a copy of an unpublished report with Franklin's latest findings on DNA. Wilkins had given them other data, too. Franklin had no idea that they had this information. Now, with the evidence from her X-ray photos and data on DNA, there was just one piece of the puzzle left to solve.

Watson had a sudden flash of genius. He worked out how the chemicals in DNA fitted together. By March he and Crick had completed a successful model of the structure of DNA.

SO NEAR BUT YET SO FAR

Meanwhile, at King's College, Franklin had almost solved the DNA puzzle all by herself. She was sure that DNA was in the shape of a helix. She had worked out nearly everything, except for how the chemicals in DNA fitted together.

In February 1953 she was probably only weeks away from the solution. In fact, twenty years later, her friend Aaron Klug found a scientific paper she had written that proved just how close she was to success. She had planned to publish this paper, dated 17 March 1953, in the scientific journal, *Nature*. It contained most of the evidence for DNA's structure.

ABOVE: *Crick (left) and Watson (right) relaxing over a cup of coffee shortly after finding out the structure of the DNA molecule. They both continued to have successful careers in science.*

But on 18 March, news of Crick and Watson's model of DNA reached King's College. The pair reported that they had discovered the structure of DNA, and were quickly writing a paper. The work they had done was certainly impressive. Yet why didn't they suggest publishing a joint paper with Franklin? After all, they had received the X-ray photographs and data from her. But for some reason the two young scientists decided not to do this.

On 25 April Crick and Watson's paper about their DNA model was published in *Nature*. They did not say that their evidence came from Franklin, or thank Franklin and Wilkins for providing information. Wilkins, Franklin and Gosling published supporting papers, which backed up the DNA model as correct. James Watson and Francis Crick had secured their place in scientific history, leaving the King's College team behind.

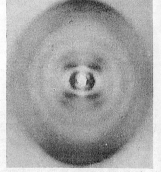

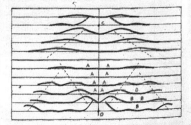

RIGHT: *The first page of the article that Crick and Watson published in* Nature *on 25 April 1953.*

A Fresh Start

'I do not remember her feeling that she had lost a competition, only that something exciting had been discovered.'

ROSALIND FRANKLIN'S SISTER, JENIFER GLYNN, 1996.

Goodbye to King's College

AS SOON AS FRANKLIN saw the DNA model at Cambridge she was impressed. She knew it was correct, which isn't surprising since it was based on her own work. As a scientist, she was delighted to see a problem solved.

Franklin now made plans to leave King's College and move to Birkbeck College. Randall told her sternly that she could not carry on working on DNA in her new job. She was even banned from having any contact with Raymond Gosling. (However, the pair cheerfully ignored this. Gosling needed Franklin to help him finish his PhD. Then they continued to work together, and published some joint papers on DNA.) To add insult to injury, Wilkins planned to repeat Franklin's work from the last two years.

LEFT: *Rosalind Franklin looking through a microscope, probably at Birkbeck College. While at Birkbeck she built up a working group of excellent scientists. She also made useful contacts with fellow scientists overseas, especially in the USA.*

Franklin was not angry about what had happened. But then she never knew just how much Crick and Watson had used her work to produce their perfect model.

A breath of fresh air

In March 1953, Franklin started work at Birkbeck College with J.D. Bernal. Bernal was a Communist, who supported the Soviet Union. Franklin didn't share his views, but she was pleased that he was determined to treat men and women equally. He was willing to accept female students and tried to encourage women in their careers. Franklin got on quite well with him. The atmosphere at Birkbeck College was a breath of fresh air after the misery of the King's College years.

ABOVE: *Dorothy Hodgkin (right) next to John Desmond Bernal at the opening of a new building of the German Academy of Sciences in 1962. Bernal was a good scientist and Franklin had great respect for him.*

WORKING ON VIRUSES

Franklin's new job at Birkbeck was to work on viruses. She began by doing X-ray work on a plant virus called Tobacco Mosaic Virus (TMV). TMV was the first virus to be worked on in a detailed way, so this was an exciting project. Once scientists understood the structure of one plant virus it would help them to find out about others. It would also be relevant to the study of animal viruses, such as foot and mouth disease. These viruses caused huge problems for farmers.

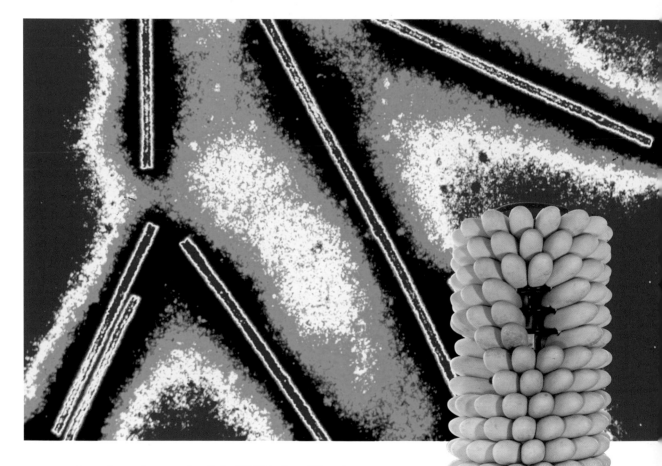

ABOVE: *A modern photograph of the TMV virus. The virus enters the tobacco plant's cells and alters its DNA so that it produces more of the virus. The plant may die as a result.*

RIGHT: *Franklin's model of the TMV virus.*

Although Franklin was an expert scientist, she worked in terrible conditions. Her tiny lab was in a run-down attic flat on the fifth floor of a building in Torrington Square, London. There was no lift and the lab had a leaky roof. Franklin had carefully placed pots to catch the drips when it rained. These things didn't bother her in the slightest – she wasn't fussed about working in comfort.

She was generally happy at Birkbeck College and got along quite well with everyone around her. However, there were occasional problems. In 1955, the British Agricultural Research Council refused to give her the grade of Principal Scientific Officer because she wasn't 'distinguished' enough. The Council then stopped giving her funding for her work. Franklin was annoyed. She felt that these people didn't want to fund a project that had a woman directing it.

Franklin made the most of her free time. She enjoyed cheap travel and adventurous holidays. Going climbing was one of her favourite activities. While at Birkbeck she travelled to Israel in the cheapest, most uncomfortable part of the boat. Her friends thought she was crazy! But Franklin liked travelling with little money so that she had to rely on her wits. For her, these were good times.

RIGHT: *Franklin on holiday in the Alps, on one of her climbing expeditions.*

IN THEIR OWN WORDS

'I was amazed, and asked why that room was not assigned [given] to a younger person, and why such a prominent [leading] scientist must work in the worst conditions. Rosalind did not complain…'

KATARINA KRANJC, A CRYSTALLOGRAPHER FRIEND OF FRANKLIN'S, WRITING TO ANNE SAYRE IN 1970 ABOUT THE CONDITIONS FRANKLIN LIVED IN.

AN UNTIMELY END

Franklin had three excellent years at Birkbeck College between 1953 and 1956. She was a happy, confident woman in her mid-30s, doing well in her job and enjoying a good social life. She liked going to parties and was always full of life.

All Franklin's friends saw her as a thoughtful and helpful person. When her doctor friend, Mair Livingstone, and her newborn baby needed somewhere to stay, Franklin moved out and let them have her flat. She even provided a cot and a pile of nappies.

In 1954 Aaron Klug, a young South African, joined Franklin in the lab. Like Franklin, he was bright and eager, and loved a good debate. They worked together extremely well.

BELOW: *Aaron Klug working in his laboratory in 1982, the year in which he was awarded the Nobel Prize for Chemistry.*

IN THEIR OWN WORDS

'She noticed everything. The fact that she produced the best specimens of TMV wasn't due to chance, or simple mechanical skills. It's an art, doing this.'

AARON KLUG ABOUT FRANKLIN, 1970.

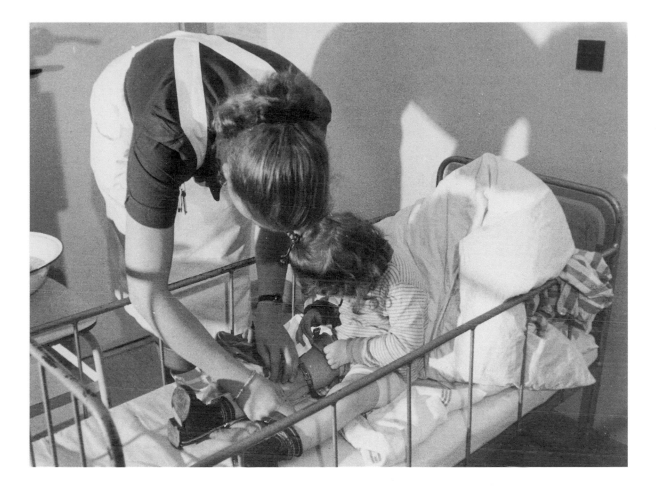

In the summer of 1956, Franklin fell ill with cancer of the ovaries. After an operation in September she said she was cured. She wasn't. Yet she threw herself into her job as usual. In the last few months of her life she began research on the deadly polio virus. It was extraordinarily dangerous to work on. She alarmed her mother once by putting a thermos flask of the polio virus in her fridge! Franklin was determined to continue working.

Even just before she died, Franklin was full of plans for the future. She hoped to go to a conference on the study of plant diseases in Bloomington, Indiana, USA, in the summer of 1958. There was also an invitation to work in Caracas, Venezuela, for six months. But on 16 April 1958 her life was cut short. She died, aged only 37.

ABOVE: *This child caught polio in the outbreak that swept Copenhagen, Denmark, in 1952. Two years on, she could not walk without callipers — splints that supported her legs. A vaccine to stop people from catching polio was introduced in 1961, just a few years after Franklin's death.*

Hidden from History

FRANKLIN'S TRAGIC EARLY death cut off the career of a fine scientist. She did not receive any reward for her work on DNA. In 1962, Nobel Prizes for Medicine/Physiology went to Francis Crick, James Watson and Maurice Wilkins. Rosalind Franklin was forgotten.

The Double Helix

Franklin lost her rightful place in history for another reason. Whether a person makes history or not depends on who writes it. The most famous book about the discovery of DNA's structure was written by James Watson. Called *The Double Helix*, it was published in 1968. Watson told a thrilling story about the 'race' for DNA, which became a bestseller.

ABOVE: *The Nobel Prize winners of 1962 in Stockholm, Sweden, after receiving their awards. You can see Maurice Wilkins (left), Francis Crick (third from left) and James Watson (second from right).*

In *The Double Helix*, Watson described Franklin – 'Rosy', as he alone called her – as a hardworking loner who disliked her colleagues. She was the plain woman in glasses who didn't know how to do her hair. (She only occasionally wore glasses in fact, and was actually quite attractive.)

Watson also criticized Franklin as a scientist. He said she was a woman who didn't know her place, which was to work for Wilkins. Many people who understood Franklin's work felt that Watson painted this picture to play down her vital role in the discovery of DNA's structure, and make his own sound more important. Other scientists also left Franklin out of their writings. For example, Linus Pauling wrote that Wilkins had produced the B form photos of DNA. If Franklin had been alive, she might have received credit for her achievements.

IN THEIR OWN WORDS

'...there was no denying she had a good brain. If only she could keep her emotions under control, there would be a good chance that she could really help him.'

JAMES WATSON'S VIEW OF FRANKLIN'S RELATIONSHIP TO WILKINS, *THE DOUBLE HELIX*, 1968.

LEFT: *A scientist working on DNA in a hospital in London, England, in 2000. In the late 1960s, there were still few women in the labs and scientific work was seen as a male job. This may have been one reason that Franklin didn't receive the recognition she deserved.*

Franklin's Legacy

Setting the record straight

THERE IS NO DOUBT that Franklin played a vital part in discovering the structure of DNA. Crick and Watson simply could not have built a correct DNA model without her data.

Yet it was Franklin's friends and fellow workers who had to remind people of her achievements. In 1962, the Science Museum in London put a model of the DNA molecule on display. Franklin's name was missing from the list of people who had helped to discover its structure. Mair Livingstone made sure that the museum added her name.

After *The Double Helix* was published, Aaron Klug wrote well-researched articles to prove the importance of Franklin's work. A biography by Franklin's friend Anne Sayre, *Rosalind Franklin and DNA* (1975), and a BBC Horizon film called *Life Story* followed. These helped to keep the memory of her work alive.

BELOW: *A protester against genetically modified (GM) crops – crops that have had their genes changed – in a sweetcorn field in France, 1998. GM crops grow well, which can be good for farmers. But they can cause problems for wildlife. No one knows what the effects of changing genes might be in the long term.*

In 1993, King's College finally recognized Franklin's DNA work. Her name appeared on a plaque along with others from King's College who had written papers on DNA. A building was named after Franklin and Wilkins, and there is also a Rosalind Franklin Building at Newnham College. In 2002, a Franklin medal was created to raise the profile of women scientists.

Franklin's other work had lasting importance, too. Her studies of coal structures are still used today and her work on TMV helped to form the basis of virus research.

But it was Franklin's DNA work that helped to revolutionize the science of genetics. Scientists have now mapped all the genes in the human body – an amazing feat. They can change plant genes to make crops grow better, produce human insulin in bacteria and do many other amazing things. Rosalind Franklin should be remembered for the important part she played in opening up the remarkable world of genetics.

BELOW: *A cystic fibrosis patient is helped by her physiotherapist. In future, genetic diseases such as cystic fibrosis may be cured by gene therapy.*

GENETIC DISEASES

The gene that causes cystic fibrosis was discovered in 1990. A couple who are planning a baby can have a simple test to find out whether they carry the gene. If they both have it, there will be a risk that their child will have cystic fibrosis. Scientists are also trying to find a way to correct problem genes. They hope to be able to cure people with genetic diseases such as cystic fibrosis. This is called gene therapy.

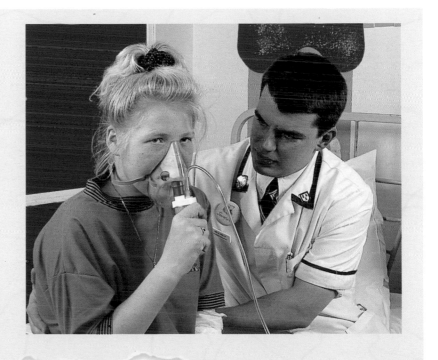

Timeline

1912
German scientist Friedrich Knipping discovers X-ray crystallography.

1914
The First World War begins.

1917
The Russian Revolution. The USA joins the First World War.

1918
The First World War ends. Women householders over 30 are given the vote in Britain.

1920
25 JULY: Rosalind Franklin is born in London. The Prohibition law forbids the making and selling of alcoholic drinks in the USA.

1922
The Union of Soviet Socialist Republics is formed.

1924
Britain has its first Labour government. The US economy is booming.

1926
Two million workers join a General Strike in Britain against wage cuts for miners.

1928
All women over 21 are given the vote in Britain.

1929
The Wall Street Crash in the USA; the Depression begins and many people lose their jobs.

1931
Franklin goes to St Paul's Girls' School.

1933
The Nazi Party wins the elections in Germany. In the USA, Franklin D. Roosevelt brings in the New Deal to provide jobs.

1935
Franklin decides she wants to be a scientist.

1938
Franklin starts her degree at Newnham College, Cambridge. Western scientists find out how to split the atom to create energy. During the war they work out how to use this energy to make atom bombs.

1939
The Second World War breaks out.

1941
Franklin gets her degree, and begins a research scholarship under Ronald Norrish. The USA enters the Second World War.

1942
Franklin is given the job of assistant research officer at the British Coal Utilization Research Association.

1944
Scientists begin to realize that the genes are in DNA.

1945
SUMMER: Franklin finishes her PhD. AUGUST: The USA drops atom bombs on Hiroshima and Nagasaki in Japan. SEPTEMBER: The Second World War ends.

1946
The Cold War between the USA and the USSR begins.

1947
FEBRUARY: Franklin moves to Paris to work at the Central State Chemistry Laboratories. Women at Cambridge University are awarded proper degrees, equal to men's.

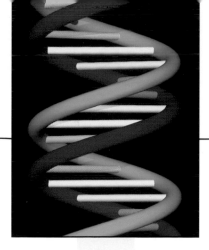

1948

English crystallographer, Dorothy Hodgkin, makes an X-ray photo of Vitamin B_{12} and works out its structure.

1950

DECEMBER: Professor John Randall offers Franklin a job working on X-ray crystallography at King's College, London. She starts work at the beginning of 1951.

1951

NOVEMBER: Franklin gives a talk at King's College in which she describes her results on DNA so far.

1952

DECEMBER: Crick and Watson get a copy of a report with Franklin's unpublished findings on the structure of DNA.

1953

JANUARY: In the USA, Linus Pauling writes a paper on the structure of DNA. It is wrong.
28 FEBRUARY: Crick and Watson complete a correct model of DNA.

17 MARCH: Rosalind Franklin prepares a paper with her DNA results to publish in *Nature*.
18 MARCH: News of Crick and Watson's correct model for the structure of DNA reaches King's College, London.
LATE MARCH: Franklin starts work at Birkbeck College.
25 APRIL: Crick and Watson's paper about the discovery of DNA's structure is published in *Nature*, with supporting papers by Franklin, Gosling and Wilkins.

1954

Aaron Klug comes to Birkbeck College to work with Franklin.

1956

Franklin becomes ill with cancer. First non-military nuclear power stations are opened in Britain.

1957

First non-military nuclear power stations are opened in the USA.

1958

16 APRIL: Franklin dies.

1961

Crick, Sydney Brenner and others work out how cells 'read' the genetic code.

1962

Crick, Watson and Wilkins share the Nobel Prize for discovering the structure of DNA.

1964

Dorothy Hodgkin wins the Nobel Prize for Chemistry.

1968

The Double Helix, by James Watson, is published. It describes the 'race' to find the structure of DNA.

1969

Dorothy Hodgkin works out the structure of insulin.

1975

A biography of Franklin, *Rosalind Franklin and DNA*, is published by her friend Anne Sayre.

1990

The gene that causes cystic fibrosis is discovered.

2000

Scientists working on the Human Genome Project work out that humans have about 30,000 genes.

Glossary

Atoms the smallest parts of all the things around us.

Bacteria tiny living things that are neither plants nor animals. They live in air, water and soil, and in living and dead plants and animals. They are vital to life but can also cause disease.

Biochemistry the scientific study of the chemistry of living things.

Cells nearly all plants and animals are made up of cells. The simplest are made up of only one cell.

Conference a large meeting in which people with the same interests can discuss their views.

Crystal a small piece of a substance with many even sides, which is formed naturally when the substance becomes solid. For example, when water freezes, it forms crystals of ice.

Cystic fibrosis a serious illness that some people are born with. It stops the lungs and other organs inside the body from working properly. Some people with cystic fibrosis die young.

Data facts or pieces of information that are collected and used to find out things.

Diabetes an illness caused by the lack of a chemical called insulin, which controls the amount of sugar in the blood.

DNA the chemicals inside plant and animal cells in which the genes are found.

Evidence the facts or things that make you believe that something is true. For example, the evidence from Franklin's DNA photos showed that DNA was in the shape of a helix.

Feminist a person who believes that women should have the same rights and opportunities as men.

Fuel anything that makes heat or power, usually when it is burnt. Examples are coal and wood.

Funding money that is given for a special purpose.

Genes the things inside the cells of living things that control what they will be like, for example, in humans there are genes for eye, skin and hair colour.

Helix a shape like a spiral.

Householders people who own or rent the home that they live in.

Insulin a chemical made by the body that is needed for good health. Insulin can be created to give to people whose bodies cannot make enough naturally.

Journal a magazine that deals with a particular subject: for example, *Nature* is about science.

Laboratory a room that is used for scientific research and experiments.

Molecule the smallest part of things after the atom. Molecules are made up of a group of atoms.

Nobel Prize a prize that is given each year to the people who have done the best work in science and writing, and those who have helped to make peace.

PhD the abbreviation for Doctor of Philosophy. It is a high-level university degree that is given to somebody who has done research in a particular subject.

Plaque a flat piece of stone or metal, with a name and dates on it. It is fixed to a wall in memory of a person or event.

Polio a disease that can paralyse parts of the body.

Scholarship money given to somebody by an organization to help pay for their studies.

Scientific paper a piece of writing about a scientific subject that is for other scientists to read.

Structure the way in which the parts of something are put together. For example, the walls, floor and roof make up the structure of a house.

Supervisor the person who helps a student and guides his or her work.

Virus a living thing, too small to be seen without a microscope, that causes diseases that people, animals or plants can catch from each other.

X-ray crystallography a way of sending X-rays through crystals to make X-ray photographs that show the structure of the crystal.

Further Information

BOOKS FOR OLDER READERS

How to Clone a Sheep by Hazel Richardson (Oxford University Press, 1999)

Genetics by Adam Hibbert (Franklin Watts, 2000)

Science Fact Files: Genetics by Richard Beatty (Hodder Wayland, 2001)

BOOKS FOR TEACHERS

Cambridge Women: 12 Portraits by Edward Shils and Carmen Blacker (Cambridge University Press, 1996). Chapter on Rosalind Franklin by Jenifer Glynn.

The Double Helix by James Watson (Penguin, 1999)

Rosalind Franklin and DNA by Anne Sayre (reissued by Norton, 2000)

PLACES TO VISIT

The Science Museum
Exhibition Road
South Kensington
London SW7 2DD
Tel. 0870 870 4771

WEBSITES

The BBC Local Heroes programme website has a good biography of Rosalind Franklin, although it gives a false impression of her parents' attitude to university education for girls; they were keen for all their children to be educated equally.
http://www.bbc.co.uk/history/ programmes/local_heroes/biogs/rsfranklin. shtml

The How Stuff Works website has information about how things work, including cells.
http://www.howstuffworks.com

The Human Genome Project website has an excellent online leaflet for children about gene-related issues.
http://www.ornl.gov/hgmis/ publicat/genechoice/contents.html

The Science Museum website has an online exhibition, 'Who am I?', about what it means to be human.
http://www.sciencemuseum.org.uk

The BBC has a website dedicated to genetics at:
http://www.bbc.co.uk/genes

Index

Numbers in **bold** refer to pictures and captions.